EERIE
ISLANDS

by Alex Giannini

Consultant: Debbie Felton
Professor of Classics
University of Massachusetts
Amherst, Massachusetts

BEARPORT
PUBLISHING

Minneapolis, Minnesota

Credits

Cover, © Kim Jones, © musicman/Shutterstock, and © Triff/Shutterstock; 3, © kwest/Shutterstock; 4-5, © Kim Jones, © 7ynp100/Shutterstock, and © Mykola Mazuryk/Shutterstock; 7, © doleesi/Shutterstock; 8, © Albert Russ/Shutterstock; 9, © doleesi/Shutterstock; 11, © LouieLea/Shutterstock; 11b, © Lancelot Speed/Wikimedia Commons/Public Domain; 12, © Yavuz Sariyildiz/Shutterstock; 13, © StockWithMe/Shutterstock; 13b, © leolintang/Shutterstock; 15, © Marco De Lauro/Getty; 15b, © Gearstd/Shutterstock; 15c, © May_Chanikran/Shutterstock; 16, © Georgios Kollidas/Shutterstock; 17, © Realy Easy Star/Toni Spagone/Alamy; 17b, © Alan Sheldon/Shutterstock; 18, © f11hpoto/Shutterstock; 19, © Chicago Bureau / FBI/Wikimedia Commons; 20, © Sivapoom Yamasaki/Shutterstock; 21, © Katia Edmundson/Shutterstock; 21b, © Elnur/Shutterstock; 21c, © Elnur/Shutterstock; 23, © Aleksandar Todorovic/Shutterstock; and 24, © triocean/Shutterstock.

President: Jen Jenson
Director of Product Development: Spencer Brinker
Editor: Allison Juda
Designer: Micah Edel
Cover: Kim Jones

Library of Congress Cataloging-in-Publication Data

Names: Giannini, Alex, author.
Title: Eerie islands / by Alex Giannini.
Description: Minneapolis, Minnesota : Bearport Publishing Company, [2021] | Series: Tiptoe into scary places | Includes bibliographical references and index.
Identifiers: LCCN 2020002398 (print) | LCCN 2020002399 (ebook) | ISBN 9781647471729 (library binding) | ISBN 9781647471781 (ebook)
Subjects: LCSH: Haunted islands—Juvenile literature. | Ghosts—Juvenile literature.
Classification: LCC BF1475.5 .G53 2021 (print) | LCC BF1475.5 (ebook) | DDC 133.1/29—dc23
LC record available at https://lccn.loc.gov/2020002398
LC ebook record available at https://lccn.loc.gov/2020002399

For more information, write to Bearport Publishing, 5357 Penn Avenue South, Minneapolis, MN 55419. Printed in the United States of America.

CONTENTS

EERIE ISLANDS

It's a perfect island day with the bright sun above and the warm sand below. It's perfect, that is, until you feel somebody watching you. You feel a tap on your shoulder and turn to look around at the empty island beach. Maybe you aren't alone after all.

Get ready to read four
terrifying tales about eerie
islands . . . if you dare.

HANGING DOLLS

The Island of the Dolls, Mexico City, Mexico

Just south of Mexico City, there's a place known as The Island of the Dolls. Hundreds of plastic baby dolls hang from trees on the island.

Some of them are missing arms or legs, while others have no eyes. The hanging dolls are very creepy, but the island's past is truly haunting.

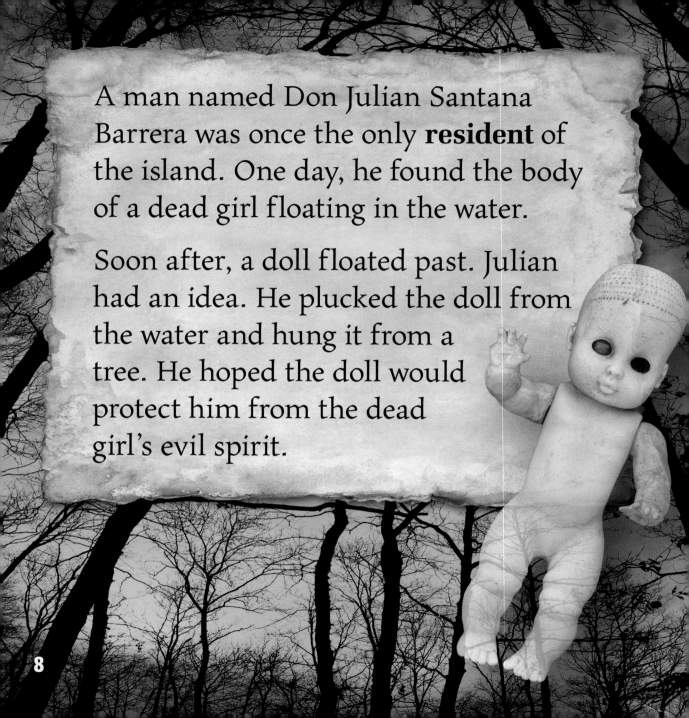

A man named Don Julian Santana Barrera was once the only **resident** of the island. One day, he found the body of a dead girl floating in the water.

Soon after, a doll floated past. Julian had an idea. He plucked the doll from the water and hung it from a tree. He hoped the doll would protect him from the dead girl's evil spirit.

Julian hung dolls in the tree for nearly 50 years until the day he died—in the same place where he first found the girl's body.

HAUNTED CASTLES

The Isle of Skye, Scotland

The Isle of Skye has been the site of bloody battles and centuries-old mysteries. Ghosts and fairies are said to roam two of its castles.

Dunvegan Castle was once home to the MacLeod family. Now, ghostly music echoes through its empty rooms.

Legend says music comes from a flag that was given to the MacLeods centuries ago by fairies. It's known today as the Fairy Flag of Dunvegan.

The remains of the Fairy Flag of Dunvegan Castle

Duntulm Castle is the island's other haunted landmark. The castle lies in ruins today. But its **gruesome** history has lived on as the spirits of Duntulm still linger.

The castle is said to be haunted by the ghost of Hugh MacDonald, a prisoner who was **tortured** and starved to death. Some still hear his deathly groaning today.

THE WORLD'S MOST HAUNTED ISLAND

Poveglia Island, Venice, Italy

Sitting in Italy's Venice Lagoon is a small island called Poveglia. Today, the island is **abandoned** and visiting it is illegal. Why? Because Poveglia may be the most haunted island in the world!

When the **bubonic plague** struck Venice in 1348, victims were **quarantined** on Poveglia. Over 150,000 people died there. Their restless spirits bring a sense of dread to the land.

A hospital at
Poveglia Island

15

Even worse, an asylum for the mentally ill was built on the island in the 1920s. Some claim the head doctor performed gruesome experiments on his patients.

One day, the doctor himself went mad. He leapt to his death from the bell tower! Even though the tower was taken down many years ago, locals still hear bells chiming on Poveglia.

The French military leader Napoleon Bonaparte once used Poveglia to store weapons. He knew his enemies would stay away from the spooky island!

AL CAPONE'S GHOST

Alcatraz Island, San Francisco, CA

Alcatraz Island is home to America's most **infamous** prison. Opened in 1934, Alcatraz held some of the world's most dangerous criminals.

One of the prisoners was Al Capone, a **notorious** Chicago criminal. The prison closed in 1963, but legend suggests Al Capone—and other inmates—still haunt the cells at Alcatraz.

Al Capone

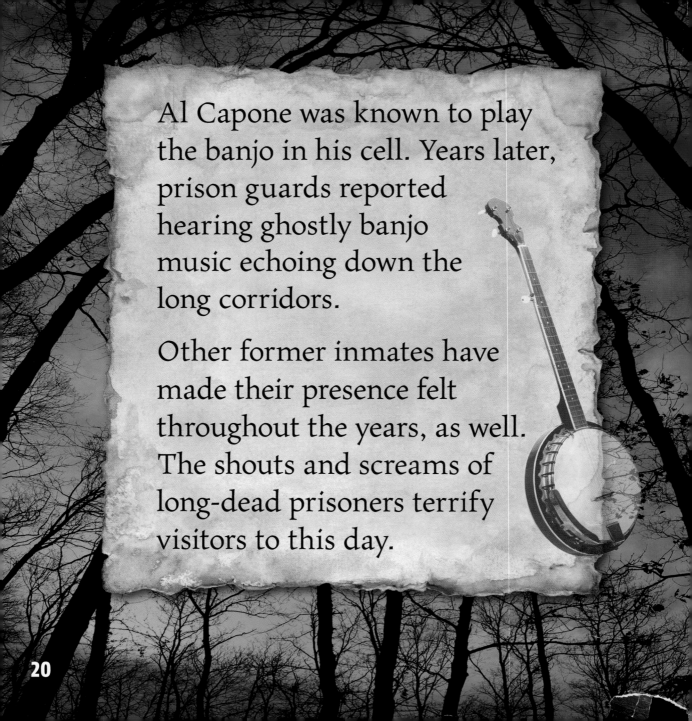

Al Capone was known to play the banjo in his cell. Years later, prison guards reported hearing ghostly banjo music echoing down the long corridors.

Other former inmates have made their presence felt throughout the years, as well. The shouts and screams of long-dead prisoners terrify visitors to this day.

Throughout its history, Alcatraz held more than 1,500 dangerous criminals. How many of their ghosts still haunt the prison?

EERIE ISLANDS
AROUND THE WORLD

ALCATRAZ ISLAND
San Francisco, California

Come face-to-face with the ghost of a dead criminal.

THE ISLAND OF THE DOLLS
Mexico City, Mexico

Discover an island haunted by the spirit of a dead girl.

THE ISLE OF SKYE
Scotland

Explore a beautiful island . . . with two creepy castles.

POVEGLIA ISLAND
Venice, Italy

What hides on the world's most haunted island?

Arctic Ocean

EUROPE

NORTH AMERICA

ASIA

Atlantic Ocean

AFRICA

Pacific Ocean

Pacific Ocean

SOUTH AMERICA

Indian Ocean

Atlantic Ocean

AUSTRALIA

Southern Ocean

ANTARCTICA

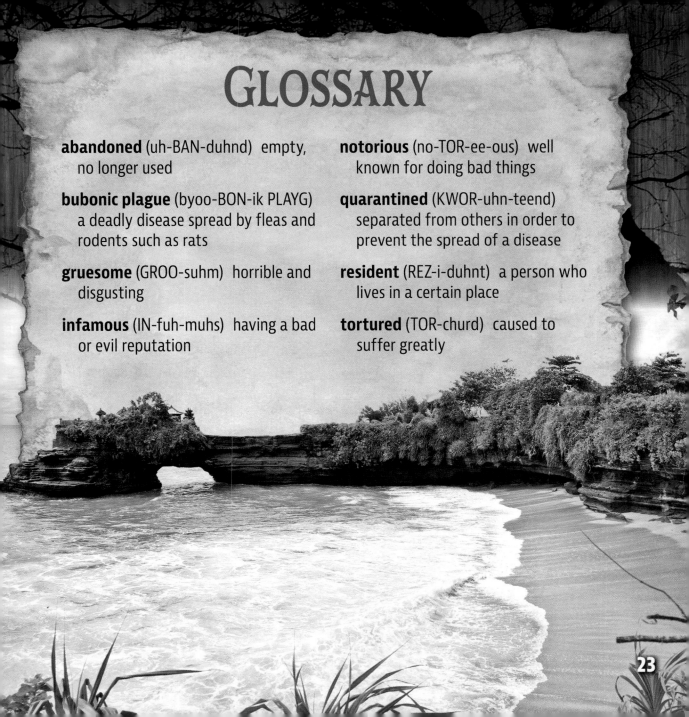

GLOSSARY

abandoned (uh-BAN-duhnd) empty, no longer used

bubonic plague (byoo-BON-ik PLAYG) a deadly disease spread by fleas and rodents such as rats

gruesome (GROO-suhm) horrible and disgusting

infamous (IN-fuh-muhs) having a bad or evil reputation

notorious (no-TOR-ee-ous) well known for doing bad things

quarantined (KWOR-uhn-teend) separated from others in order to prevent the spread of a disease

resident (REZ-i-duhnt) a person who lives in a certain place

tortured (TOR-churd) caused to suffer greatly

INDEX

READ MORE

Markovics, Joyce. *Chilling Cemeteries (Tiptoe Into Scary Places).* New York: Bearport (2017).

Phillips, Dee. *Nightmare in the Hidden Morgue (Cold Whispers II).* New York: Bearport (2017).

LEARN MORE ONLINE

1. Go to **www.factsurfer.com**
2. Enter "**Eerie Islands**" into the search box.
3. Click on the cover of this book to see a list of websites.

ABOUT THE AUTHOR

Alex Giannini is a writer who also works
in a public library. In his free time, he likes
to hunt for thrilling ghost stories.